THE WORLD WAR ONE

GRANDMA'S PHOTOGRAPH

A One Act Play

Alan Marshall

Published by Playstage
United Kingdom.

An imprint of Write Publications Ltd

www.playsforadults.com

Designed by Kate Lowe, Greensands Graphics
Printed by Creeds Ltd, Bridport, Dorset

Note to producers about staging "Grandma's Photograph".

The play is set in a small photographic studio over a three year period: 1914 – 1916. Very little changes physically – except the clothing of the characters and some of the props/backcloths that the photographer uses to put behind the clients for the shots.

What does change is the demeanour of the characters with the passing of the years. As they come for their first photograph, the PYE family are very jolly, full of patriotic fervour, and this is matched by MR STOTT. MRS STOTT, however, is more subdued about the situation but this is, partly, because she is rather dominated by her husband and finds life frustrating. When the second photograph is taken, MR and MRS PYE's son is dead and MR STOTT's brother has been killed, so everyone is in a very sober mood. MR STOTT, particularly, is in the grip of a depression which he cannot seem to shake off. When the final photograph is taken, both MRS PYE and MRS STOTT have been widowed. Whilst MRS PYE is filled with anxieties about how she is going to cope in the world without a man, MRS STOTT, on the other hand, has been liberated and displays a new-found confidence. To SARAH PYE, the situation causes her some bitterness, initially, because she has lost her fiancée and realises that lower middle class women can no longer expect to be stay-at-home wives. But when she learns that MRS STOTT has achieved her dream of being a photographer without any disapproval from society, she begins to find new hope.

This play was created because of a set of photographs of my own relatives which I found amongst my grandmother's belongings after she died. (The photographs are reproduced on the next page.) They show my great uncle's family – one photo at the beginning of the war, when they were all proud and happy and one photo at the end of the war, when he is dead and his wife is left to bring up two small children on her own. They were reproduced on postcards, ready to send to the relatives (in this case, my grandmother). It would be a nice dramatic touch if, when this play is performed, similar photos were taken of the cast, in the three stages of family destruction, and they were projected on to the flats or a screen at the end of the play, to show the audience how the drama would be viewed through the eyes of the "Grandma" who received the annual photographs.

Costumes
All instructions about costumes are within the text of the play. However, for research purposes we recommend the following websites: www.cosetsandcrinolines.com and www.fashion-era.com

Props
The backdrop which is used behind the customers posing for their photographs, depicts various interior and exterior scenes and they should be on a stand or screen so that they can be flipped over and changed when required. Rather like a giant flip chart.
Make sure that all props – toys, the camera etc. are of the period.
For research purposes we recommend the following websites:
www.licm.org.uk
www.photographica.nu
www.antiquewoodcameras.com
(Note: a fake camera can easily be constructed.If you look at cameras of the period they are mostly a wooden box, bellows and a brass lens. If you fix the black cloth permanently to the front of the camera, then very little of the actual camera will be seen.)

Music
There are many CDs that contain the music of the Great War era. One we would particularly recommend is *Your Country Needs You* by River Records, available to order from all good music shops and Amazon.

THE WORLD WAR ONE SERIES.
No.2: GRANDMA'S PHOTOGRAPH

CAST *(In order of appearance)*

MR STOTT	Photographer, hardworking and cheerful man, if a little domineering towards his wife, aged 50+
MRS STOTT	His wife, also hardworking but subdued, aged 50+
MR PYE	Railway clerk, outgoing personality, aged late 50s
MRS PYE	His wife, a little anxious, conscious of her 'position' in society, aged 50+.
JOHN PYE	Their son, newly signed-up to the Army, excited. Aged mid-20s.
SARAH PYE	Their daughter. Proud of her brother. Newly engaged. Bubbly personality. Aged 28-30 in the play.

3 female and 3 male parts.

The action takes place in MR STOTT's small photographic studio, in the years, 1914, 1915 and 1916.

WORLD WAR 1. No.2.
GRANDMA'S PHOTOGRAPH

SCENE 1. 1914.

MR STOTT's photographic studio. It has three walls and the two side walls are angled outwards towards the audience. (SEE SET PLAN) Upstage centre right is the door. Stage right is the "posing area" where customers sit, or stand, to have their photographs taken. At the moment this consists of a backdrop on a stand, depicting a lake scene; two wooden chairs; a white half column, on which is an arrangement of flowers. In the front of the stage, facing the "posing area" is a camera of the period, on a wooden tripod, with a black cloth covering it. There is a table next to the camera on which are black drawstring bags, cardboard labels, a pencil and extra glass photographic plates. The upstage wall has various props along the bottom, which MR STOTT uses for the customers, such as toys for children, plinths and vases and extra chairs. The stage left wall contains a large window, through which daylight is streaming.

MRS STOTT is busy removing the plinth and flower arrangement from the posing area, while MR STOTT is saying goodbye to the previous customers through the half-open door.

MR STOTT   …Goodbye Mrs Jones…goodbye. Ah! Hello, Mr Pye…Mrs
                Pye… I shan't keep you a moment. We're just adjusting the
                scene. *(MR STOTT closes the door and comes back into the
                room.)*

MRS STOTT   I've taken away the floral arrangement and plinth. Shall I
                leave the two chairs?

MR STOTT	*(sighing and a little irritable)* Why do you do these things, Evie, without asking me first?
MRS STOTT	Sorry, Arnold.
MR STOTT	Well, I suppose it will do. The two gentlemen can stand. We won't bother with the lake scene though. I think just the plain blue will be best.

(MRS STOTT flips over a plain, pale blue, backdrop and smooths it out. MR STOTT puts a new plate in the camera.)

MRS STOTT	Have we photographed them before?
MR STOTT	Once. Last year. The husband's some high up clerk in the railway offices, I think. The wife, if I remember, gives herself some airs. It's always the way with the families of these minor officials. They think they're a cut above the rest of us. *(indignantly)* I mean, that Parsons woman, this morning, saying to me, "Oh, Mr Stott, I expect people in trade, like yourself, will be making money out of this war, what with all the photographs people will want now." I mean – trade – as though I was a coalman or something! Who do these people think they are?
MRS STOTT	She didn't mean anything by it, Arnold. What else would she call us, anyway? She's not the sort of woman who would know the word "artisan".
MR STOTT	I take exception to that word as well! A blacksmith is an artisan. A photographer is an artist.
MRS STOTT	*(sighing)* Whatever you say, Arnold.
MR STOTT	Are we ready?
MRS STOTT	All ready. I'll go and fetch them. *(MRS STOTT opens the*

door and speaks.) Mr and Mrs Pye, Mrs Stott is ready for you now, if you'd like to come through.

(The PYE family enter. MR PYE is dressed in his best suit with an uncomfortable looking stiff collar and tie; MRS PYE is dressed in a long summer frock and is wearing her best straw hat with flowers on; SARAH is wearing a blouse and long skirt, her hair is up in the style of the day. She is wearing white gloves and carrying a parasol. JOHN PYE is dressed in the uniform of an ordinary soldier.)

MR STOTT	*(switching on his best affable persona)* Oh, I see that someone has done his patriotic duty! May I shake your hand, young man! *(He goes forward and shakes JOHN's hand enthusiastically.)* I expect I shall see more young men in uniform but I must say that you have the distinction of being the first in this studio, Master Pye.
SARAH	Is he really!? How exciting, John!
MR PYE	He just got kitted out yesterday.
MRS PYE	Yes. We were hoping that he would have his uniform in time for the annual photograph.
SARAH	Grandma will be so thrilled!
MR STOTT	Ah, it's for Grandma, is it?
MRS PYE	Yes. My mother. She lives in Berkshire and I don't see her as often as I would like but she's always had a photograph every year, since we were married.
MR STOTT	Most commendable, Mrs Pye. Most commendable. We stood and watched the parade yesterday, of all the young men who had signed up. I dare say you were marching in it, were you, Master Pye?

JOHN	Absolutely! Me and all my friends. We all signed up together last week.
MR STOTT	Wanted to be the first to fight for your country, sir?
SARAH	John always wants to be the first! He's so impatient!
JOHN	*(joking)* I say, Mr Stott! That's not a German camera, is it? I hear that the Hun makes pretty good cameras.
MRS STOTT	*(speaking without thinking)* Yes, they do, sir. The best...
MR STOTT	*(snapping)* Evie, that will do! *(remembering himself and smiling at the PYEs)* Rest assured, Master Pye, I wouldn't have a German camera in the studio...despite my wife's opinion of them. No, this camera *(he rests his hand on the top)* is British through and through. It's a Triple Victo, made by Houghtons Limited, in London. The biggest camera factory in the UK. My late father-in-law, who originally owned this studio, had a preference for German cameras... but I wouldn't give them house-room, sir – wouldn't give them house room.

(MRS STOTT looks depressed.)

Now...(MR STOTT *moves away from the camera and begins shepherding the PYE family into a group in the posing area)* if you would like to sit here, Mrs Pye, and your daughter next to you...may I say what a lovely hat you are wearing, Mrs Pye! The colours are quite vibrant. Perhaps, Mr Pye, you might consider investing just a little extra money in a hand-painted photograph. My wife does the hand-painting and she is quite meticulous.

MRS PYE	Oh yes, Herbert! Do let's have a painted photograph!
MR PYE	Very well, m'dear. It will save you having to describe your

hat in the letter to your mother.

MR STOTT   Excellent! Excellent. Now, Mr Pye, if you would like to stand behind your wife and Master Pye, if you would just stand to the side of Miss Pye, so that we can see the full extent of your uniform, please.

(MR STOTT goes back to his camera, puts his head under the black cloth and looks through the camera.)

(muffled voice from under the cloth) Good, good.

(MRS STOTT, unable to contain herself any longer, taps MR STOTT on the back. He emerges, irritated.)

What is it?

MRS STOTT   *(speaking quietly)* The photograph will be unbalanced. It would be much better if the father stood out as well and we put a flower arrangement in between the two men.

MR STOTT   *(whispering angrily)* Evie! I've told you before! Don't interfere!

MRS STOTT   *(whispering back defiantly)* It would look better and we can charge more for the photograph if I have to paint the flowers as well.

MR STOTT   *(glaring at her but having second thoughts. He then turns to the PYE family with a smile and speaks loudly)* A slight change of positioning is needed! *(He goes over and gently pulls MR PYE out of the group to stand behind but to one side of his wife.)* There! That looks more balanced! *(briskly)* Evie! Would you bring over the floral arrangement on the plinth, please?

(MRS STOTT brings over the plinth and then the floral arrangement and places them between the two PYE men)

MRS STOTT	*(to MRS PYE)* I shall paint the flowers to match the very pretty flowers on your hat, Mrs Pye.
MRS PYE	Why, thank you! How kind.
MR STOTT	*(resuming his position under the black cloth)* Oh, yes. That looks much better. *(MRS STOTT's facial expression betrays the fact that she knew it would look better anyway.)*
SARAH	I do hope that I don't ruin the picture by closing my eyes when the flash light goes off. I just can't seem to help it.
MR STOTT	*(coming out from under the black cloth)* No need to worry about that, Miss Pye. We don't use a flash in this studio.
JOHN	*(surprised)* You don't? I thought all photographers used flash lights?
MR STOTT	I would if I were taking a photograph of someone in their own home but here in the studio with the skylight *(he points upwards)* and the large south facing window *(he points to the window in the wall)* we make use of natural light. It gives altogether a softer and more natural photograph.
MR PYE	Makes sense to me. It's like the difference between gas and electricity. They've just changed all the lighting in the railway offices where I work to electricity. The lighting is much too harsh now. Gives me a headache. I much preferred the old gas lighting.
MR STOTT	Ah, yes. The new ways are not necessarily better, are they? *(changing the subject)* Right, now. I think we're ready. Evie, if you would stand by, please. *(MRS STOTT picks up a black cloth bag and comes forward to her husband's elbow. MR STOTT goes under the black cloth.)* Now, everyone very still please! *(The PYEs remain perfectly still. MR*

STOTT comes out from under the cloth and takes the lens cap off the camera. He then raises his hand towards the PYEs signalling them to remain very still, mentally counts to five, then puts the lens cap back and drops his hand.) And... everybody relax! Now, if you would just wait while I change the plate and we will take another picture.

(MR STOTT fiddles about under the black cloth and MRS STOTT reaches in and takes the plate from him straight into the black bag. She then steps to one side, pulls the draw string of the bag and picks up a cardboard label on a string, writes a name on it and attaches it to the drawstring. MR STOTT loads up another plate into the camera. He chats while performing this operation.)

So, Master Pye, when do you sail for foreign parts?

JOHN   Three days time. Can't wait to get at the Boche. Just a bit worried it will be all over before I get there. The reports are that the Austrians, particularly, are pretty useless, and the worry is that they might capitulate before I actually get in position in France.

MR PYE   I shouldn't be surprised at all, John, my boy. The whole thing's a lot of German hot air, if you ask me. But you mustn't be too disappointed. The main thing is that you are seen to be eager to do your bit.

MR STOTT   Hear, hear! I would join up myself but I am the sole breadwinner here. Makes it a bit awkward. Don't know how Mrs Stott would manage if I were away.

(MRS STOTT gives him a sideways look and then shakes her head to herself as if she can't believe he said such a thing.)

However, my brother has volunteered. He's joined the Gloucesters. He'll have to be the one to do his bit for the family.

SARAH My fiancée has joined up too. He's going to be in the same regiment as John.

MRS PYE Yes. George and John have always done things together, ever since they were boys. Best friends, you know.

MRS STOTT *(suddenly chipping in)* I think this war will be very hard on the womenfolk.

(They all look at her in astonishment. There is a momentary pause where no-one can think of a rejoinder.)

MRS PYE *(uncertain)* Well…yes…I suppose you might be right, Mrs Stott. Perhaps the lower classes might find it a bit of a struggle without a man's full wage coming in to the house.

SARAH *(with mock horror)* Mother! I've never heard you talk about wages before! Isn't that a little vulgar?

MRS PYE *(flustered)* Oh dear!...well..I'm sure I didn't mean…

JOHN Sarah's only teasing you, mother! Don't take everything so seriously!

MR STOTT *(glaring at MRS STOTT)* Yes, well, sir – I'm afraid that's a failing of the fair sex – isn't it? Taking things far too seriously. Now! We're ready for another photograph. May I ask you to pose once more, please? Evie! *(motioning her over.)*

(MR STOTT goes under the black cloth again. MRS STOTT is ready with another black bag. The whole procedure is repeated, as before. MR STOTT comes out from the cloth and removes the lens cap.)

That's good. Just a few more seconds....fine.

(They perform the plate removal and MRS STOTT takes it to one side to label the bag.)

So, Mr and Mrs Pye, all done! I presume you will want postcards made?

MR PYE   Yes, please. We would like twelve. *(To MRS PYE)* It was twelve, wasn't it, dear?

MRS PYE   Yes. But can we have two of them hand-painted? One for my mother and one for my sister.

SARAH   Oh, mother, can't we make it three? I would like to give one to George before he leaves for the front.

MRS PYE   Oh for goodness sake, Sarah! George doesn't want to carry around a picture of the whole family! We must have a portrait done of you on your own.

MR PYE   Capital idea! Would you be able to do it now, Mr Stott?

MR STOTT   I'm sorry, Mr Pye, but there is another family waiting outside. Perhaps we could make an appointment for the end of the week? Would that be soon enough?

JOHN   Yes, George won't be leaving for France for two weeks, Sarah. That gives you plenty of time.

MR STOTT   Evie! Bring the appointment book!

(MRS STOTT brings the appointment book and scans the pages.)

MRS STOTT   The earliest we could do is Thursday morning at 11 'o'clock.

MRS PYE   That would be fine, wouldn't it, Sarah?

SARAH   Yes, fine. Mother! Shall I be photographed in evening dress?

I want to look my very best.

MRS PYE   Well, I don't know…you can't possibly travel from home, during the day, wearing an evening dress. That would be most improper.

MRS STOTT   We do have a changing room, Mrs Pye. Your daughter could bring her evening dress and I could help her dress her hair.

MRS PYE   *(relieved)* Oh yes! That would be much more suitable! Thank you, Mrs Stott.

(MRS STOTT writes it in the book.)

MR STOTT   *(shepherding the PYEs towards the door)* Good. That's settled then.

MR PYE   *(extending his hand)* Thank you very much, Mr Stott, for being so accommodating. When will the photographs be ready?

MR STOTT   *(shaking MR PYE's hand)* In two days time, sir. Our delivery boy will bring them round to your house.

MR PYE   Excellent. Well, goodbye.

MR STOTT   *(extending his hand to JOHN PYE, who shakes it)* And good luck, sir. Please take our best wishes to the front with you.

JOHN   Thanks, old man.

(The PYEs leave. MR STOTT closes the door and his personality changes as he speaks to MRS STOTT.)

MR STOTT   Well! You surpassed yourself today, Evie Stott! What was all that misery about? *(mimicking her voice, sarcastically)* "It'll be hard on the womenfolk" That's not what customers want to hear! And offering to dress that girl's hair, as though you were some ladies' maid! What were you thinking of? You mind your tongue in future!

MRS STOTT   *(sullenly)* I'm fed up with minding my tongue.

MR STOTT   And don't keep interfering when I'm taking photographs...

MRS STOTT   *(defiantly)* My father was a damn sight better photographer than you'll ever be. And I was brought up to know the craft as well as any man. I have a right to my opinion.

MR STOTT   *(sharply)* Not in front of the customers, you don't! Your father may have been a good photographer but it's my name above the door now – not his. And you are my wife and you will do as I say! Do you understand?

MRS STOTT   *(quietly but firmly)* You only inherited this studio because you married me. Unfortunately, my father died before The Married Women's Property Act became law, so you persuaded him to will it to you. If he'd have lived a year longer, the studio would have been mine, and it would have been my name above the door.

MR STOTT   Well he didn't and it's not. So hard luck. Now, you can just put your Suffragette ideas back in your silly little brain and start setting up for the next customers. *(MR STOTT walks over to the door and pauses before opening it.)* I'm warning you, Evie. Keep your mouth shut, or you can stay at home and behave like a proper wife. *(He opens the door and puts on his 'jolly' persona)* Mr and Mrs Thomas! Lovely to see you! Oh, and young Master Thomas too. Evie! Get some toys ready!

(The lights fade to black. Music starts. "YOUR KING AND COUNTRY WANT YOU." This continues until actors are ready for Scene 2.)

SCENE 2. 1915.

The lights go up to reveal MR STOTT sitting on a chair by the back wall, hunched over and looking a bit dazed. He is not himself, as we discover later. MRS STOTT comes in to the room through the door. She is wearing much the same clothes but she has added two white pull-on sleeve protectors, which have some dark stains on them. The flower arrangement has changed. Instead of a bright array of flowers, it is now a bunch of white lilies.

MRS STOTT   *(gently but firmly)* Arnold? *(he doesn't react so she speaks sharply)* Arnold!

MR STOTT   *(gathering his senses)* Yes?

MRS STOTT   The next customers have arrived. Are you feeling up to it?

MR STOTT   *(getting up but moving a little slowly, as though he has aged somewhat)* Yes, yes of course I am. Who is it?

MRS STOTT   The Pye family.

MR STOTT   Pye? Oh yes, the father's a clerk at the railway office, isn't he? The son is in the Army.

MRS STOTT   *(matter-of- factly)* There's no son anymore. At least I presume not. They're in mourning.

MR STOTT   *(sadly)* Oh, not another one. That's the third this week.

MRS STOTT   *(unsympathetic)* Mm. Well, what do you expect? It's the men who start the wars and the women who pay the price. What do men think war is going to be like? Some schoolyard game, where no-one gets hurt? What backcloth shall we have?

MR STOTT   *(half-heartedly)* You choose.

MRS STOTT	*(talking to herself whilst changing the backdrop)* Seems to me that I'm doing all the 'choosing' lately – and the developing – and much else besides…
MR STOTT	*(irritable)* Yes, well I've not been myself. You know that.
MRS STOTT	*(going towards the door and pausing)* It's been five months since your brother got killed, Arnold. Time you were on the mend, don't you think? *(He turns away from her, his face a picture of misery)*
MR STOTT	He was my only brother, Evie. And he was so young…
MRS STOTT	*(twisting the knife a little)* Mm. And he wouldn't have joined up if you hadn't egged him on.
MR STOTT	I know, I know. You don't have to keep reminding me.
MRS STOTT	*(taking a certain amount of grim satisfaction from adding to his misery)* Seems to me that a lot of people need reminding of how much they pressured young men to join in with this foolishness. Most of the young girls in this country should hang their heads in shame for encouraging their sweethearts to join up. And most of the fathers, or older brothers, in your case, should never forgive themselves for bullying their young sons, or brothers, into going to fight.
MR STOTT	*(anguished and raising his voice)* Leave me be, Evie! For God's sake!
MRS STOTT	Keep your voice down! Do you want to frighten away the customers? Now, pull yourself together! There's plenty of people grieving nowadays. You don't have to wallow in it. Now, I'm going to open the door. Compose yourself Arnold. *(he makes a concerted effort to pull himself together while she opens the door and smiles)* Mr and Mrs Pye! Please come through!

	(MR and MRS PYE enter, followed by their daughter, SARAH. MRS PYE is dressed all in black, with a black hat with feathers. MR PYE is dressed in a suit, with a black armband. SARAH is dressed as a nurse, also with a black armband. They look solemn.)
MR PYE	*(going up to MR STOTT and shaking his hand.)* Good day, Mr Stott, I'm afraid we meet under less pleasant circumstances this year. My son…John…was killed in France two weeks ago. So our family is much reduced.
MR STOTT	I am deeply sorry, Mr Pye. I know how you feel. My dear brother was also lost to us.
MR PYE	Ah. Then we are kindred souls, Mr Stott. Kindred souls. *(MR PYE walks over to his family and the two women automatically sit in the posing area in the chairs they occupied before. MR PYE stands behind and between the two women.)* Will this suffice?
MR STOTT	Yes. That will be fine.
MRS STOTT	*(speaking with reverence)* Many bereaved families choose to have the display of lilies in their photograph. Would this be your wish, Mr Pye?
MR PYE	*(looking at his wife)* What do you think my dear?
MRS PYE	*(holding back the tears)* Yes. Put the lilies where dear John stood for last year's photograph. I think it would be fitting.
	(MRS STOTT nods and brings over the plinth, then fetches the vase of white lilies, placing both behind and just to one side of SARAH. MR PYE moves to the outer side of his wife, as he was in the first photograph.)
MRS STOTT	Begging your pardon Mr Pye, but it would be better if you

stood centre back, otherwise there will be a large gap in the centre of the photograph.

SARAH   *(ironically)* There will be a large gap anyway – now that John has gone.

MR PYE   Of course there will, my dear. *(He pats her on the shoulder and stand in the centre, as before.)* Should I stand here?

MRS STOTT   Yes, that will be fine.

(She notices that MR STOTT is staring at the floor, as though he can't remember what to do next.)

Excuse me one moment. *(She goes over to MR STOTT and speaks quietly but firmly to him.)* Arnold. The customers are ready.

MR STOTT   What? Oh...yes.

(He moves towards the camera mechanically, as though disinterested, and goes through the motions of looking under the black cloth. Then he emerges again.)

(distractedly) That seems fine.

MRS STOTT   *(hastily)* Let me just check. *(She goes under the black cloth and then temporarily reappears.)* That plinth needs moving in a couple of inches. Might I impose upon you, Mr Pye, to just move it towards you a little?

(She disappears under the black cloth while MR PYE obligingly moves the plinth a couple of inches in towards the centre. Then she re-emerges.)

Thank you, sir. I'm sorry to have to ask you. Mr Stott is not himself today.

(She goes up to MR STOTT, puts her arms round him, leads

him back to the chair on the back wall and sits him down.)

There, Arnold. You just sit there for a bit. *(She turns back to the PYE family)* I'm sorry, Mr and Mrs Pye but Mr Stott has been unwell since the death of his brother. It hit him hard, you see. They were very close.

MR PYE   I quite understand. Shall we come back another day?

MRS STOTT   Goodness, no. I'm perfectly capable of taking the photograph, Mr Pye. In fact, I'm probably better qualified than my husband. My father, you see, owned this business first and he taught me all he knew. My husband was his apprentice for five years but I was my father's apprentice for twenty five years. I trust you have no objection to my taking the photograph?

MR PYE   *(undecided)* Well...

SARAH   For goodness sake, father! Lots of women are doing men's jobs now!

MR PYE   Well, sadly, yes. That's not to say that I approve, of course. But, well...needs must, I suppose.

MRS PYE   Please let's just get on with it, Henry. It doesn't matter a jot who takes the photograph!

MR PYE   Of course dear. Please carry on, Mrs Stott.

MRS STOTT   Thank you, sir.

(MRS STOTT takes a black plate bag off the table and comes round to the side of the camera. MR STOTT, meanwhile, has put his head in his hands and seems lost in depression.)

Right. If you would be so kind as to keep completely still, please...

(She takes the lens cap off, mentally counts to five and then replaces it. The PYE family do not smile at all for this photograph.)

I'll just change the plate and then we'll take another. *(MRS STOTT goes under the black cloth, removes the plate and puts it in the bag. She then emerges and deftly labels the bag. Then she inserts another plate.)*

SARAH   I must say, you certainly seem to know what you're doing, Mrs Stott.

MRS STOTT   Thank you, miss. Like I said, I had a lifetime of training from my father. How are you coping with being a nurse?

SARAH   Well, I'm only an auxiliary and the training is very hard but I'm beginning to feel that I may have an aptitude.

MRS PYE   God forbid! No decent woman in her right mind would want to be a professional nurse. Some of the things they have to do and see are positively indecent.

MR PYE   Hear, hear. If it wasn't for the fact that we are at war...

SARAH   *(interrupting impatiently)* Exactly! We are at war. Everyone has to do their bit. Of course I won't become a professional nurse. Nurses aren't allowed to marry and I intend to marry George as soon as he is discharged from the Army. But, meanwhile, I'd rather be nursing than some of the other jobs that were on offer. I mean Millie Henshaw is driving an omnibus, for God's sake!

MRS STOTT   Right. We're ready for another photograph. If I could just ask you to keep still...

(The PYE family freeze, whilst MRS STOTT goes through the procedure of removing the lens cap, mentally counting to

five and replacing the lens cap. They then relax as she removes the plate into another bag and labels it.)

There we are. All done. Will you be wanting postcards and how many? Oh, by the way, we don't do hand painted photographs any more.

MRS PYE Well there wouldn't be much point in hand painting us this time. It would be rather drab.

MR PYE I suppose we'd better have the usual twelve copies, Mrs Stott.

(MRS STOTT writes it in the book.)

MRS STOTT I'm afraid that, at the moment, I am doing all the developing, as well as mostly everything else, so I shan't be able to get the photographs to you until the end of the week.

MR PYE That's alright. We're not in any rush.

MRS PYE You must be finding it hard to cope...

MRS STOTT No, madam. I thrive on hard work. Besides, I'm sure that Mr Stott will be better soon. *(speaking to MR STOTT)* Won't you, Arnold?

MR STOTT *(Taking his head out of his hands)* Eh? What's that, my dear?

MR PYE *(speaking slightly louder as though MR STOTT is deaf)* Your wife says she hopes you will be better soon, Mr Stott, and so do we.

MR STOTT *(not quite comprehending)* Yes. We're kindred spirits, Mr Pye. We've both lost someone dear to us. *(He puts his head back in his hands.)*

MRS PYE *(quietly)* Poor man. Some people cannot bear up under grief.

SARAH Has he seen a doctor, Mrs Stott?

MRS STOTT	No, miss. One hardly likes to bother doctors when they have so many physically wounded men to deal with.
SARAH	True.
MRS STOTT	He'll perk up, eventually, I expect. Let me see you out. *(MRS STOTT shepherds them towards the door and opens it for them.)* Good bye, Mr and Mrs Pye. Miss Pye. I hope to see you again under happier circumstances.
MR PYE	Good bye, Mrs Stott.
MRS PYE	Good bye, my dear.
SARAH	Good bye.

(They leave and MRS STOTT closes the door with a sigh of relief. She turns back into the room and talks to herself.)

MRS STOTT	So now I'm taking the photographs as well. Good. It's what I should have been doing all along. *(She goes over to MR STOTT)* Come along, Arnold. There are no appointments for an hour. I think you should go home to bed.
MR STOTT	*(passively)* Yes, Evie. I'm so tired, you know. I...I can't think.
MRS STOTT	I know, Arnold. You need to rest. Come along.

(She takes his arm and leads him out. Light fades to black. Music swells. "KEEP THE HOME FIRES BURNING". This continues until the actors are ready.)

SCENE 3. 1916.

The lights go up. Nothing has changed in the photographic studio. The door is slightly open and we hear MRS STOTT's voice offstage.

MRS STOTT   *(offstage)* Do go through, ladies. I shall be with you in just a moment....

(MRS PYE and SARAH enter. SARAH is still dressed as a nurse but without the black armband and with a different nurse's hat and a red belt. MRS PYE is dressed in a simple long skirt and blouse and is wearing the flowery hat she wore for the first photograph.)

MRS PYE   It does seem strange to be back here again. It brings back such awful memories. *(She sits down on one of the chairs in the posing area and blows her nose.)*

SARAH   Now, mother. I don't think the memories are awful at all. Coming here should remind you of the good times we had as a family. I'm glad that we have the photographs to remind us, frankly.

MRS PYE   I shall never get used to losing John. I can hardly bear to look at the photographs of his dear smiling face. And now... thirty two years of marriage – snuffed out, just like that and I must get used to being a widow. I don't think I ever shall.

SARAH   *(firmly)* Well you'll have to, mother - just as I will have to get used to being a spinster.

MRS PYE   Oh, don't say that, Sarah! Once this war is over...and George is... better...you'll be married, of course you will.

SARAH   *(sighing)* How many times do we have to go over this?

George will *never* get better. He has severe shell shock. The doctors say he will never recover his wits. The man who sits and rocks himself backwards and forwards in complete silence in the asylum is not the George that I became engaged to. Once and for all, mother…I will never marry George. Neither will I get married to anyone else, as long as this war carries on. They said in the newspaper, just yesterday, that if the rate of casualties persists, when the war is finally finished, there will be at least four women for every one man. I'm already thirty years old, so there is no hope for me. Anyway, I'm not going to marry out of desperation. No, I shall stay a nurse. I have an aptitude for it. Besides, we need the money.

MRS PYE   *(distressed)* Oh, don't dear…don't talk about money…it's so…

SARAH   Vulgar? Times have changed, mother and so have our circumstances. Father left you a small amount to live on when he died and we have no other man to bring money into the house. Now that I am a staff nurse, I earn enough money to allow us to live as we always used to – give or take a few economies.

MRS PYE   *(touching her hat)* Yes, I know. No more new hats. Oh dear! Do you think Mrs Stott will remember that I wore this hat two years ago?

SARAH   I shouldn't think so, at all. Judging by the wall out there, crammed with photographs, Mr Stott seems to be doing a roaring trade. I should think that his wife struggles to even remember our names, given that we only come here once a year.

(MRS STOTT enters, carrying a bouquet of flowers. She is wearing an artist's overall over her skirt and blouse (see Notes to Producers) and has an air of breezy confidence.)

MRS STOTT   I do think that hat is very pretty, Mrs Pye. I liked it the very first time I saw it.

MRS PYE   *(dismayed)* Oh…er…thank you.

SARAH   I see that you have been very busy, Mrs Stott, judging by the number of photographs you have on display. Is your husband recovered?

MRS STOTT   *(breezily)* Oh no, Miss Pye. Arnold died not long after you had your last photograph taken.

SARAH   Oh, I'm so sorry!

MRS STOTT   *(busying herself with checking the plate bags and the camera)* Yes…well. There was nothing that could be done for him. He just turned his face to the wall, as they say. The doctor said he died of a broken heart. Foolish nonsense, if you ask me. Whoever heard of such a thing? Mind you, I've never seen a man decline so quickly and he was wracked with guilt because it was he who pressured his brother into signing up. Once he heard that his brother had been killed he seemed to age overnight.

MRS PYE   I have been widowed too, Mrs Stott. My dear husband had a heart attack four months ago. Just keeled over. It was over in a second.

MRS STOTT   Oh, I am sorry, Mrs Stott – but at least it was mercifully quick.

MRS PYE   Oh yes. It was that alright.

SARAH	So, Mrs Stott, you've been doing all this photography by yourself?
MRS STOTT	I certainly have. Trade has never been so brisk. I've also invested in a field camera and I've been doing some work for the local newspaper as well.
SARAH	Goodness, you must be a bundle of energy!
MRS STOTT	*(busying herself with the camera)* Ah, well – all those years to make up for, I suppose. My husband wouldn't allow me to do anything at all, except hand paint the photographs. You can't imagine how galling it was to paint some of the awful portraits my husband took. He wasn't a very good photographer, at all.
MRS PYE	*(concerned)* Dear me. Was he not?
MRS STOTT	Competent, I think is the word. He was a competent photographer. He had no artistic flair. A lot of photography is about artistic composition, you know. And lighting.
SARAH	Yes. I was looking at some of the photographs on your wall outside. Very beautiful portraits indeed. You obviously do have artistic flair, Mrs Stott. Tell me…the large one in the centre of the wall…is that a picture of the actress Sybil Thorndike?
MRS STOTT	It is. She's a very good friend of mine, in fact. I shall be taking portraits of many of the actors at the Old Vic Theatre next week.
SARAH	How thrilling! How did you become friendly with Miss Thorndike?
MRS STOTT	Through my work for the local newspaper. Miss Thorndike was opening a new library and I took her picture there.

MRS PYE	You do seem to be very busy, Mrs Stott. Do you have any help at all in running your business?
MRS STOTT	Well, not exactly. I've employed a local woman to come in twice a week and do all my accounts and paperwork.
MRS PYE	Another woman!?
MRS STOTT	Well, there aren't any men available, are there, Mrs Pye? One has to search for competence amongst the female population now.
SARAH	Exactly. Just as I was telling my mother earlier. There will be a great many spinsters, once this war is over, and they will want to be trained to do something.
MRS STOTT	Well, they could start by campaigning to get the vote, in my opinion.
MRS PYE	*(worried)* Are you a radical, Mrs Stott?
MRS STOTT	*(firmly)* Indeed not, Mrs Pye. I am simply a businesswoman who like to have her say in the way the country is run. You can rest assured that once women get the vote there will be no more wars and senseless deaths.
SARAH	*(delighted)* Absolutely!
MRS STOTT	Now. I think we're ready. If you would just adjust your uniform, Miss Pye, and turn your body so that you face slightly in towards your mother...Would you like an arrangement of flowers behind you?
MRS PYE	Yes, that would be nice...but not the lilies. We don't want to send my mother another reminder of death.
MRS STOTT	No, quite. We must all put our best foot forward now, mustn't we? Present a positive face to the world.

(She goes to the vase of lilies, removes the flowers and replaces them with the bouquet she brought into the room. Then she places the plinth and then the vase between and a little behind the two PYE ladies.) There we are! Much more jolly. I think I'll change the backdrop as well. *(She flips over another backdrop which simply has a striped wallpaper pattern.)* There! It makes it look like your own drawing room. *(She goes back to the camera and disappears under the black cloth.)* Perfectly still now. A little smile, if you would please....

(The PYE ladies smile. MRS STOTT comes out from the cloth, takes the lens cap off, mentally counts to five and then replaces it.) I'll change the plate and then we'll have another photograph. *(She goes through the system of changing the plate, whilst talking.)* Hopefully, I shan't have to go through all this rigmarole for much longer. The Americans have invented sheet film, would you believe, which will replace the heavy glass plates. It sounds wonderful and I shall be the first to try it out, when it appears.

SARAH   But will the photographs be as good? I mean my brother gave me a Brownie camera before he died – you know, one of those little ones? *(MRS STOTT pulls a face)* Yes, exactly. They're very handy but they take awful photographs really.

MRS STOTT   Well, there's a lot more to taking photographs than the amateur realises. Success all depends upon the quality of the materials and, as I said before, the lighting. None of these 'toy' cameras will ever amount to anything. Useful though, if you just want to take a few holiday snaps, I suppose. Right. Ready again? Here we go. Smiles, ladies, please! *(She takes the lens off and does the usual silent count before replacing the lens.)* And there we are. I see your uniform is slightly different, Miss Pye. Does that mean you are fully qualified?

SARAH   Oh you do have an excellent memory! Yes, I'm now a fully trained staff nurse at Queen Mary's Hospital.

MRS STOTT   Good for you! The country needs all the trained nurses it can get.

MRS PYE   *(not convinced)* Her father wouldn't have liked it, though. He always wanted to see Sarah married. It is so difficult getting through life without a man at one's side.

MRS STOTT   *(briskly)* It all depends on the man, Mrs Pye. You were lucky, it seems, in that you had a long and happy marriage. Those of us who did *not* can tell you that having no man at all is sometimes preferable to making a reluctant bargain with someone who might make you miserable.

SARAH   Very true. I was only telling mother something similar earlier. And times have changed so drastically. This war could go on for a very long time and more women shall just have to fend for themselves.

MRS STOTT   Yes. There'll be no turning back now. How many copies would you like, ladies?

MRS PYE   *(looking at SARAH)* Twelve?

SARAH   *(taking her mother's hand)* No, mother. So many people are no longer with us that I would say eight would suffice.

MRS STOTT	*(writing in her book)* Eight. No problem. The postcards will be with you in a few days. Are you still at the same address?
MRS PYE	Yes.
SARAH	*(extending her hand to MRS STOTT who shakes it)* Well thank you, Mrs Stott. *(as an afterthought)* Tell me...do you ever go to any of the Women's Suffrage meetings? In your capacity as a local newspaper photographer.
MRS STOTT	As a matter of fact I'm attending one in the Horticultural Hall next Wednesday evening.
SARAH	Might I accompany you?
MRS PYE	*(shocked)* Sarah!
MRS STOTT	Absolutely. I think you would find it very interesting.
SARAH	I've always wanted to go to a meeting but I shouldn't like to go on my own. Not the first time, anyway.
MRS STOTT	*(smiling)* There's nothing to be afraid of, you know. They're all quite nice women and all much too busy working now to have time for radical behaviour.
MRS PYE	I should hope so! I shouldn't like to think of you being tempted to throw yourself under a horse, Sarah, or tie yourself to some railings. The shame of it would kill me!
SARAH	Oh, mother, don't be so silly. I'm far too sensible for such things. Although I might be tempted to throw a rotten egg at the Prime Minister...
MRS PYE	*(appalled)* Sarah!
SARAH	I'm teasing you, mother. Don't get upset.
MRS STOTT	I shall keep an eye on her, Mrs Pye. So...Sarah...if you would like to come here at six on Wednesday evening, we

shall walk to the meeting together.

SARAH   It will be a pleasure, Mrs Stott.

MRS STOTT   Please call me Evelyn.

SARAH   A pleasure, Evelyn.

              *(The PYE ladies leave and MRS STOTT closes the door and
              smiles. The Lights fade to black. Music swells: ROSES OF
              PICARDY and photographs I, 2 and 3 of the PYE family
              are projected on to the back wall of the set.)*

THE END

FURNITURE LIST

Throughout: Backdrop on stand; two wooden chairs in posing area; white half column/plinth; arrangement of flowers in vase; camera on tripod with black cloth; extra chairs along back wall; assorted "props" for photographs (see script).

PROPERTY LIST

On stage
at start: Black drawstring bags; "glass photographic plates"; cardboard labels with string; pencils; order/appointment book; multi-coloured flower arrangement in a plain vase.

Page 3:   SARAH is carrying a parasol.

Page 9:   MRS STOTT brings appointment book and pencil.

Page 12:   Flower arrangement has been changed for a bouquet of white lilies.

Page 18:   MRS STOTT uses appointment book.

Page 20:   MRS PYE needs a handkerchief.

Page 22:   MRS STOTT enters with a bouquet of varied flowers.

Page 27:   MRS STOTT uses appointment book.

LIGHTING AND EFFECTS PLOT

Page 1:   *Opening music. Bring up lights.*

Page 11:   Cue : MR STOTT: "...Evie! Get some toys ready!"

                Fade lighting to black. Bring up music which continues until actors are ready for Scene 2.

Page 12:   *Bring up lights and fade music.*

Page 19:   Cue : MRS STOTT : "I know, Arnold. You need to rest. Come along."

                Fade lighting to black. Bring up music which continues until actors are ready for Scene 3.

Page 20:   *Bring up lights and fade music.*

Page 28:   Cue: SARAH: "A pleasure, Evelyn."

                Lights fade slowly. Bring up music. If used, all three photographs are projected on to the back wall until they are the only things visible in the darkness. Hold for a couple of seconds then fade images as the music is faded.

GRANDMA'S PHOTOGRAPH – SET PLAN

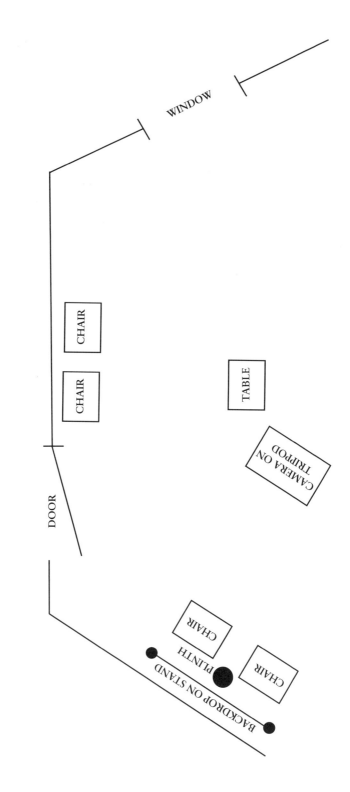